Family Matters ABC/BCP
201a Decies Road
Ballyfermot
Ph: 01 6238102

To my family and friends, to all the colours lived together – A.LL.

The Colour Monster

ANNA LLENAS

Anna Llenas was born in Barcelona. She graduated in Advertising and Public Relations at the Autonomous University of Barcelona (UAB), with a diploma in Graphic Design by The Escola de la Llotja and has a postgraduate degree in Creative Illustration from the Escola Eina. She began her career in advertising as Art Director in Bassat-Ogilvy and one day she made the decision to become a full-time illustrator. She now creates her own design projects, which she markets through different channels. She has developed graphic projects for clients as diverse as *La Vanguardia* (Spanish daily newspaper), Nestlé and the Government of Catalonia. She has collaborated with other authors illustrating their stories. This picture book is her first as both author and illustrator. Llenas has also been influenced by the Art Psychotherapy and Psychosocial training at the University Pompeu Fabra, and currently acts as a teacher and art therapist specialising in art and emotional education.

For more information go to: **www.annallenas.com**

A TEMPLAR BOOK

Published in the UK in 2016 by Templar Books,
an imprint of Bonnier Books UK
4th Floor, Victoria House
Bloomsbury Square, London WC1B 4DA
Owned by Bonnier Books
Sveavägen 56, Stockholm, Sweden
www.bonnierbooks.co.uk

El monstruo de colores was first published in Spain by Editorial Flamboyant S. L.
Copyright © Anna Llenas, 2012
English translation copyright © Templar Publishing, 2016
English language edition edited by Katie Haworth

21 20 19 18 17 16

ISBN: 978-1-78370-423-1 (paperback)

Printed in the UK

The Colour Monster

ANNA LLENAS

templar
books

This is my friend the colour monster.

Today he's all mixed up and very confused.
He doesn't know why.

Look at you,
you're all over the place!

That's because your feelings are all
stirred together, so your colours are too.

I know! Let's put each feeling
in a different jar so we can look at it
more closely. I can help if you like.

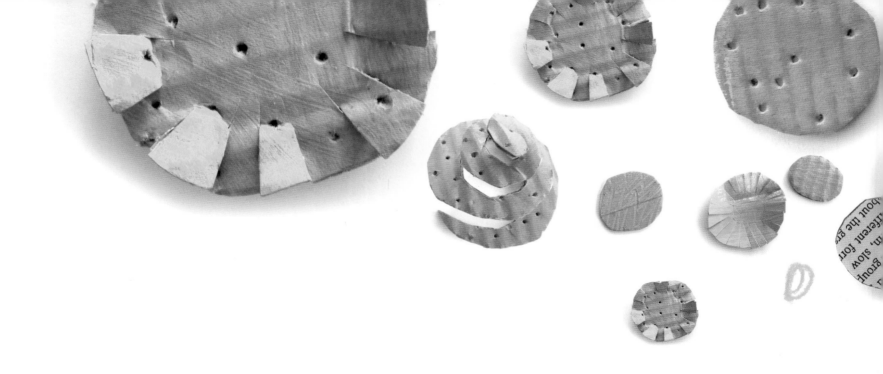

This is happiness.
It shines yellow like the sun
and twinkles like the stars.

You feel bright and light. You laugh, you jump, you dance! You want to share that feeling with everyone.

This is sadness.

It's gentle like a blue rainy day.

Sadness can make you cry.
It can make you feel alone.
But if you're sad, I'll hold your hand.

This is anger.
It blazes red like fire.

Anger can make you want to stomp . . .

. . . and **Roooooooaaaaaaarrr!**
and shout, 'It's not fair!'

This is fear.
It is black like the night
and hides in shadows like
a scaredy cat.

Being afraid can make you feel
very small and alone. If you're
scared, tell me why and we'll walk
through the forest together.

This is calm.
It's quiet like the trees
and soft like their leaves.

Now you're calm,
you breathe slowly and deeply.
Ahhhhhh! You feel at peace.

There, we've finished!
Here are your feelings,
and each one has a different colour.

Let's look at them together:

yellow

happiness

blue

sadness

red

anger

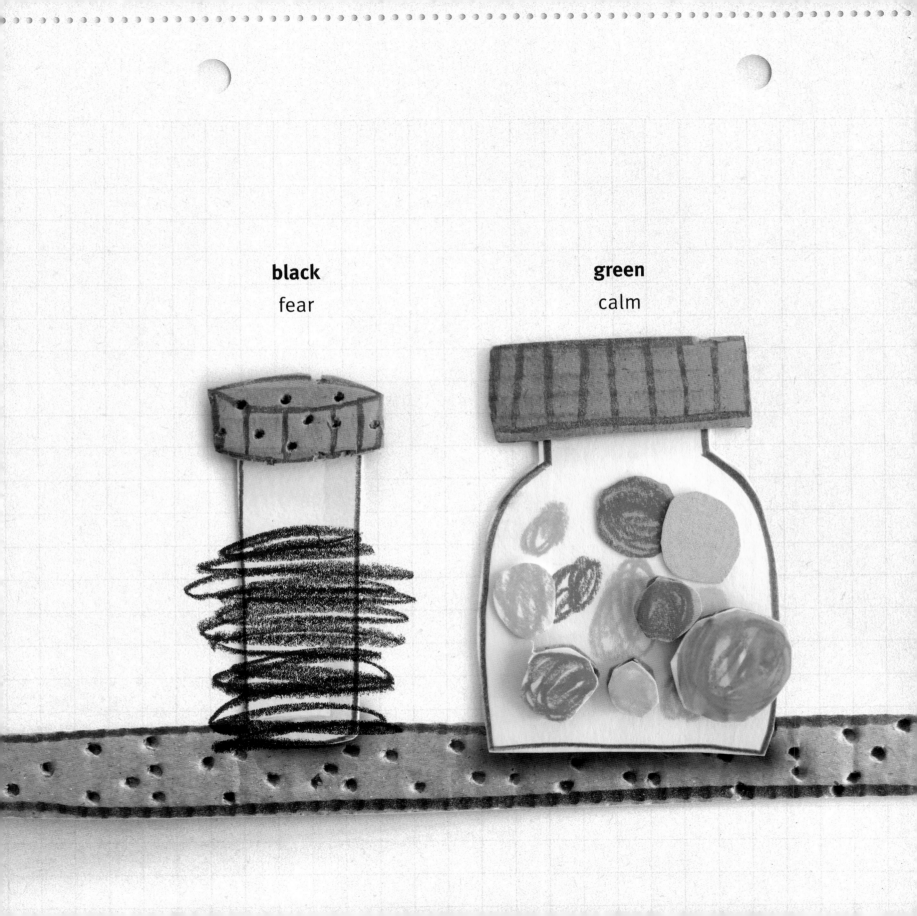

But what's this?
You look different,
Colour Monster!
Er . . . how do you feel now?